20th Century
PERSPECTIVES

The Holocaust

Susan Willoughby

Heinemann Library
Chicago, Illinois

© 2001 Reed Educational & Professional Publishing
Published by Heinemann Library,
an imprint of Reed Educational & Professional Publishing,
Chicago, IL

Customer Service 888-454-2279

Visit our website at www.heinemannlibrary.com

Designed by AMR
Illustrated by Art Construction
Originated by Dot Gradations
Printed by Wing King Tong in Hong Kong

05 04 03 02 01
10 9 8 7 6 5 4 3 2 1

Library of Congress Cataloging-in-Publication Data
Willoughby, Susan, 1945-
   The Holocaust / Susan Willoughby.
      p. cm. -- (20th century perspectives)
   ISBN 1-57572-436-7 (library binding)
   1. Holocaust, Jewish (1939-1945)--Juvenile literature. 2. Warsaw (Poland)--History--Warsaw Ghetto Uprising, 1943--Juvenile literature. [1. Holocaust, Jewish (1939-1945)] I. Title. II. Series.

D804.34 .W55 2001
940.53'18--dc21
                             00-063456

Acknowledgments
The publisher is grateful to the following for permission to reproduce copyright material:
Associated Press, p. 4; Author's photograph, p. 42; Corbis, p. 26; Dina Gottlieg, pp. 23, 24; Doris Fogel, pp. 16, 41; Hana Greenfield, p. 5b; Hulton Getty, pp. 5a, 8, 9, 11, 12, 15, 36; Margit Korestzova/The Jewish Museum, Prague, p. 21; Ullstein Bilderdienst, p. 30; USHMM Photo Archives/William Blye, p. 13; USHMM Photo Archives, pp. 14, 17, 19, 25, 28, 29, 31, 33, 34, 35, 37, 38, 39, 40, 43.

Cover photo: USHMM Photo Archives

Special thanks to Christopher Gibb for his comments in the preparation of this book.

The author would like to thank the following for their information and help: Doris Fogel, Fort Wayne, Indiana; Jeff Gubitz; and the Fort Wayne Jewish Federation, Fort Wayne, Indiana.

Every effort has been made to contact copyright holders of any material reproduced in this book. Any omissions will be rectified in subsequent printings if notice is given to the publishers.

Some words are shown in bold, **like this.** You can find out what they mean by looking in the glossary.

Contents

What Was the Holocaust?

The memorial on the wall of the Pinkas Synagogue shows the names of Holocaust victims.

A stroll through the Pinkas **Synagogue** in the old city of Prague, capital of the modern-day Czech Republic, is a journey into the past. The synagogue was founded in the Middle Ages, and over the centuries, generations of Prague's Jewish community have worshiped within its walls. Today, it has a newer and deeply significant importance, for it stands as a memorial to all the Jewish inhabitants of the former Czechoslovakia who were victims of the Holocaust—those who were taken from their homes all over the country, imprisoned, degraded and humiliated, randomly beaten or murdered, and finally deliberately **exterminated.** The visitor is faced with the enormity of the crime. On the walls of the synagogue are the beautifully carved names of 77,297 men, women, and children who so cruelly lost their lives.

You cannot see, in your mind's eye, this vast number of human beings. The task becomes even harder when you consider that the Jewish people of Czechoslovakia represent only a small proportion of the total number of their fellow Jews who perished— approximately six million from all over Europe during World War II (1939–1945). This was the Holocaust, or the Shoah as it is known in **Hebrew.** It is hardly the name of an event, but rather the word we use to describe the size and scale of this massive slaughter mainly of Jews, but also of other groups such as gypsies, **Slavs,** homosexuals, and the mentally handicapped who were considered inferior and, therefore, undesirable. The word also describes the manner in which it happened. The Holocaust was sinister, not just because of the prejudice and hatred or of the vast numbers involved, but also because it was carried out in such a planned and systematic way. It aimed at the total extermination of an entire race of people.

This was the plan of Adolf Hitler and the **National Socialist German Workers Party (Nazis)**, who ruled Germany from 1933 until 1945. Hitler began to carry out his plan in Germany almost from the moment he came to power. As his armies swept across Europe after 1939, the Jewish communities of the countries taken over soon felt the full force of his wicked policies. The result was the **ghettos, concentration camps,** and finally, the **death camps.** When the war ended and the camps were **liberated,** the world looked on in horror as the full extent of the evil crimes that had been committed behind the cloak of warfare was revealed. How could such a thing have happened? What had really happened?

This photograph shows piles of victims' bodies, following the liberation of the death camps.

To help answer some of the questions, there were the survivors. They emerged half starved, tortured, their lives shattered, their families destroyed, and their loved ones lost. They had lived through the horror. They all had stories to tell, evidence to give. For some time, though, they remained silent. Their physical wounds may have healed, but the emotional scars and the search for friends and loved ones took much longer. As time went by, the evidence began to emerge. There were records kept by brave and defiant ghetto communities, poems and paintings, many left by children and, more recently, the testimonies of those who survived. Some of these you will see and read in this book, for they tell us, in graphic and painful detail, the story of the Holocaust.

The story of Hana Greenfield

Hana was born in Kolin, Czechoslovakia. When the Nazis entered Czechoslovakia, her life changed dramatically. She had to wear the **Star of David** to indicate she was a Jew. She could not attend school or travel. She was separated from her friends. In the years that followed, she was taken to the Terezin ghetto outside Prague where she was separated from her mother, whom she never saw again. She was transported to the concentration camp of Bergen–Belsen and then to the death camp of Auschwitz where she escaped the gas chambers because she was chosen for forced labor. This meant going to Hamburg, where she and other women worked unloading ships. She survived and later went to live in Israel. She has written about her experiences and the horrors that she witnessed and endured. Her life is just one example of a victim of the Holocaust.

The Jews—A Persecuted Race

The origins of anti-Semitism

The term **anti-Semitism** is used to describe racial prejudice and discrimination shown towards Jews. This did not begin with Hitler. Its roots go back almost 2,000 years to the time when the Jews were scattered over many parts of the world. Even in the first century B.C.E., around five million Jews already lived outside their spiritual home of Palestine. Most lived within the Roman Empire. Following the destruction of Jerusalem by the Romans in C.E. 70, these numbers increased as more Jews were driven out of their homeland. They settled increasingly in the countries of Europe. Some adopted the language, beliefs, and culture of the country in which they had settled. Others continued to be identifiable as Jews and, consequently, became the victims of prejudice.

In the 14th century, Jews were often depicted showing contempt for Christianity. This illustration from Chaucer's Canterbury Tales shows a Jew throwing his child into an oven for entering a church.

"Alas! Alas!" said the Jew, "on every hand the spoilers arise against me: I am given as a prey unto the Assyrian, and a prey unto him of Egypt."

"And what else should be the lot of thy accursed race?" answered the Prior…

From the novel *Ivanhoe*, by Sir Walter Scott, set in the Middle Ages

Jewish ghettos in the Middle Ages

The character of the Jew, Isaac of York, as portrayed by Sir Walter Scott, typifies the attitude of Christians in the Middle Ages towards Jews in their communities, where they were despised. The reasons for this are mainly religious. The Jews were seen by Christians as those who had rejected Jesus Christ as the Son of God and who were responsible for his death. Many Jews, like Isaac, were wealthy. In the Middle Ages, the Roman Catholic Church forbade moneylending (usury), so when anyone needed to borrow money, they had to ask a Jew who had become rich, often because of success in trade. The Jews' claim to be God's "Chosen People" also caused resentment. So they were shunned and made to live in separate districts from Christians in most European cities. These districts were known as **ghettos.** They were made to wear a yellow badge to indicate they were Jews to the rest of the community.

The Prague ghetto

In Prague, the ghetto that clustered around the **synagogue** was typical of similar Jewish communities in European cities. It was overcrowded and enclosed. Rich and poor Jews had to live in unhealthy slum conditions. They were also vulnerable to attack. Jews were often made **scapegoats** for any calamity that struck. This led to violent attacks on Jewish communities. This discrimination lasted in Prague until the end of the 18th century. Finally, in 1850, the ghetto was destroyed because it was a health hazard. Its inhabitants were eventually allowed to live among the Christian inhabitants of the city.

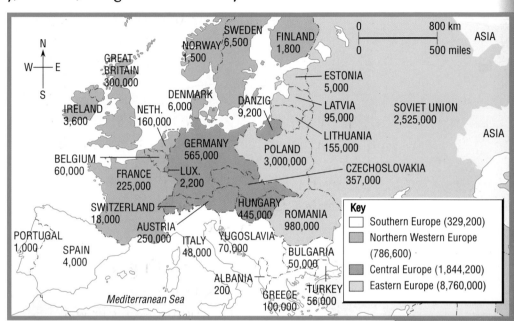

This map shows the distribution of Jews (about nine million) throughout Europe in 1933.

JEWS AND GENTILES—SOME EXAMPLES OF PREJUDICE

1096: DURING THE FIRST **CRUSADE**, JEWS WERE MASSACRED WHEN CHRISTIAN ARMIES CAPTURED JERUSALEM.

1190: JEWS IN LONDON WERE MASSACRED AS RICHARD THE LIONHEART WAS CROWNED KING OF ENGLAND. THE VIOLENCE SPREAD. YORK JEWISH COMMUNITY COMMITTED MASS SUICIDE RATHER THAN BE AT THE MERCY OF THE ANGRY **GENTILE** MOB.

1348–1349: THE BLACK DEATH PLAGUE HIT EUROPE. PEOPLE BLAMED JEWS, CLAIMING THEY HAD POISONED WELLS. THIS LED TO FURTHER VIOLENCE AGAINST JEWS.

15TH CENTURY: IN SPAIN, JEWS WERE BROUGHT BEFORE THE **INQUISITION**. SOME WERE BURNED AS **HERETICS**.

16TH CENTURY: MARTIN LUTHER, THE PROTESTANT REFORMER, SAID THAT THE SYNAGOGUES AND HOMES OF JEWS SHOULD BE DESTROYED, AND THAT JEWS SHOULD NOT BE ALLOWED TO TRAVEL ABOUT FREELY OR TO LEND MONEY.

1894: ALFRED DREYFUS WAS AN OFFICER IN THE FRENCH ARMY AND A JEW. HE WAS FALSELY ACCUSED OF TREASON. ANTI-SEMITISM IN FRANCE MADE IT VERY DIFFICULT FOR HIM TO PROVE HIMSELF INNOCENT OF THE CHARGES.

1897: KARL LUEGER WAS ELECTED MAYOR OF VIENNA. LUEGER CLEVERLY USED THE ANTI-SEMITISM OF THE VIENNESE TO MAKE SURE OF BEING ELECTED. IN PARTICULAR, HE USED THE ARGUMENT THAT JEWS WERE INFERIOR TO THE **ARYAN** RACES. LUEGER WAS STILL IN POWER IN 1907, WHEN HE BECAME THE ROLE MODEL FOR AN IMPRESSIONABLE YOUNG MAN THAT HAD JUST ARRIVED IN VIENNA. HIS NAME WAS ADOLF HITLER.

1920S: JEWISH IMMIGRANTS IN THE UNITED STATES BECAME VICTIMS OF THE KU KLUX KLAN, A RACIST ORGANIZATION THAT WANTED TO KEEP U.S. SOCIETY WHITE AND PROTESTANT.

Adolf Hitler and the Rise of Nazism

The man who was to have such an extraordinary hold over large sections of the German people was born on April 20, 1889 at Braunau in Austria, and spent most of his childhood around Linz, northern Austria. His father, Alois, was a customs officer who often lost his temper and beat his son. Hitler was devoted to his mother, Klara. He was brought up a Roman Catholic and was a choirboy at his school in Lambach. In 1907, devastated by his mother's death, Hitler went to Vienna to become an artist. He failed several times to enter the Viennese Academy of Fine Arts and spent three miserable years living in a hostel for homeless men, making a poor living by selling his paintings. During this period, his prejudice and hatred of the Jews took root. He was able to study Karl Lueger and recognize the powerful appeal of **anti-Semitism** to a lot of people.

> *"When I came face to face with Hitler, I felt that I had come face to face with God."*
>
> Reinhard Spitzy, SS officer

In 1914, when World War I broke out, Hitler was living in Munich. Here he enlisted in the German army. He was proud of Germany and its army. He served as a messenger and was awarded the Iron Cross twice for his bravery in such a dangerous job. But he was a solitary individual and one who was not considered to be officer material because he was not regarded as a leader of men. He was devastated by the German surrender in 1918. Hitler blamed the Jews and **communists,** saying that

Hitler's early life and actions are shown in this timeline from 1889–1933.

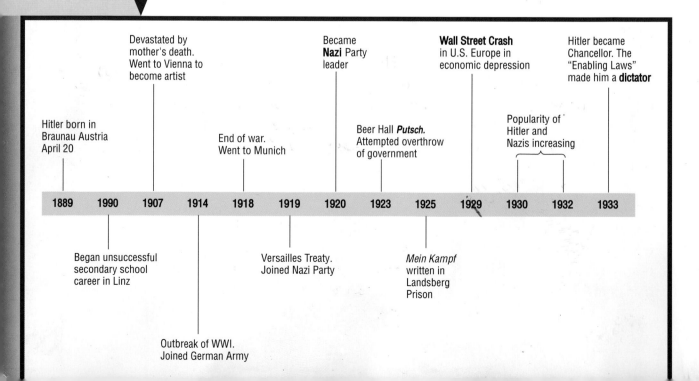

they had betrayed Germany. The German people had been stabbed in the back, he said. It was a powerful suggestion that a depressed and demoralized people were eventually pleased to believe.

After the war, Hitler became involved in politics. He discovered that he had a great ability: he was a gifted public speaker. He assumed leadership of the National Socialist German Workers Party (Nazis) and in 1923, tried to take over the government in a revolt in Munich called the Beer Hall *Putsch.* It failed and he ended up in Landsberg prison as a result.

Mein Kampf

While he was in prison, Hitler wrote his book *Mein Kampf* ("My Struggle"). He dictated it to his friend, Rudolf Hess, and read it aloud to other friends. In it, he set out his belief that the German, or **Aryan,** race was superior to all others and especially to Jews and **Slavs,** who were definitely inferior. This is what makes Hitler's anti-Semitism different from earlier times when the Jews were hated because of their religion. Hitler identified them as a race of people and not just as a religious group. He claimed that, if the Aryan race was to take up its truly superior position in the world, it had to be kept pure. Contamination by other races had to be prevented. He went on to say that the superior race needed ***"lebensraum"*** (room to live).

This photograph of Adolf Hitler was taken during his imprisonment in Landsberg, 1924.

When the book was published in 1925, people either did not understand its contents or dismissed them as the ramblings of an eccentric. Very few recognized the threat that lurked in those pages, not only to the Jews, but also to the whole of Europe. No one expected that Adolf Hitler would ever have power to carry out his ideas.

Depression!

In a normal situation, Hitler would never have come to power in Germany. But by the early 1930s, the situation was far from normal. Part of the explanation goes back to the effects of World War I. The German people had been humiliated by the surrender of their army and by the terms of the 1919 Treaty of Versailles.

When the war ended, Germany was ruined. The currency was worthless. In 1929, after a brief recovery, Germany plunged into the deepest **depression** ever known. By September 1932, over five million people were unemployed. They were desperately poor and looking for a savior. The government had no solution.

Adolf Hitler, Chancellor of Germany, is welcomed by supporters at Nuremberg, 1933.

A weak government

Since 1919, Germany had been ruled by an elected government. This was called the **Weimar Republic.** It was made up of a number of political parties which did not always agree with each other about what was needed. Workers wanted jobs. Factory owners and industrialists wanted their businesses to make profits. The government was unable to satisfy either of them. There were strikes and protests. The situation was getting out of control.

Others said that they knew how to save Germany. One group was the **Communists.** In 1917, the **Russian Revolution** had swept a Communist government into power. Communist ideas were attractive to many workers because they were promised a fair share of all the wealth that their work created. The bosses were terrified of Communism. A Communist government would take over their businesses. The only alternative to the Communists seemed to be Hitler and his **Nazi** Party.

The depression that hit Germany in 1929 gave Hitler the opportunity that he had been waiting for. He had the chance of coming to power without using force, as he had tried to do in 1923. He could get the German people to vote for him. Here his remarkable ability as an **orator** came into its own. He played on the hopes and fears of his audiences. He attacked those who had been responsible for the German surrender in 1918. He blamed Jews and Communists for accepting the terms of the Treaty of Versailles. He convinced his listeners that these people were responsible for Germany's present hardships. He lifted their spirits by telling them that they belonged to a master race and inspired them with his vision of **Aryan** domination. He could excite his audiences to frenzied adoration. His power of speech and presence made him a **charismatic** leader who appealed to all classes of people.

Hitler's rise to power

Hitler was able to convince large sections of the German population that he was indeed their savior. He could provide jobs for the workers, and restore law, order, and prosperity to Germany. Out in the streets, his "Stormtroopers" (SA) or "brown shirts," as they came to be known, toured around apparently breaking up strikes and disturbances. Invariably, the SA had really caused the trouble in the first place. Hitler also promised to make Germany a great power again.

In the Reichstag—German parliament— elections of 1928, 1932, and 1933, support for the Nazis increased dramatically although, undoubtedly, large numbers of voters were threatened or bullied into voting. On January 30, 1933, Hitler got his wish and became chancellor (head of government) of the German Republic. He used this powerful position to remove all opposition to himself and the Nazi Party. In February, the Reichstag building in Berlin mysteriously caught fire. Hitler used this to claim that there was a Communist conspiracy to overthrow the government. The German president, Hindenburg, was persuaded to pass laws banning freedom of speech and of the press. In this atmosphere, Germany went to the polls once more in March 1933. The Nazis won an even bigger victory. When the new Parliament met, Hitler demanded to be given the power to pass laws by himself. By the time President Hindenburg died in 1934, Hitler was a **dictator.**

The Reichstag building was mysteriously set on fire in 1933. A young Communist was blamed.

The Plight of Jews in Germany

Propaganda and censorship

Life in Germany changed rapidly. Hitler was determined to control the minds of all Germans. He set up a **propaganda** ministry under the direction of Joseph Goebbels. Goebbels took over the media completely to make sure that there was no criticism of Hitler and the **Nazi** Party. Instead, everything was done to build up Hitler's image and to ensure that people were loyal. Huge, well-organized **rallies,** and carefully planned film footage, newspaper, and radio coverage of Hitler all contributed to the plan. Membership of the Nazi Party became essential to securing jobs or favors. Supporters were identifiable by the **swastika** emblem they wore.

Below is the public burning of 25,000 "undesirable" books in Berlin in 1933.

They were encouraged to hang the Nazi flag from the windows of their apartments. Those who did not were easily spotted and treated as suspicious.

On May 10, 1933, libraries and bookshops were raided by Nazi gangs. They removed all the books that the Party leaders had identified as undesirable. On that night, 25,000 books were publicly burned. They included the works of Jewish writers Albert Einstein and Sigmund Freud and a number of famous American writers such as Ernest Hemingway and Sinclair Lewis.

The key, as far as the Nazis were concerned, was the control of the minds of children and young people. Teachers were expected to teach Nazi ideas, and a nationwide group called Hitler Youth was formed so that, both in school and free time, young people could be brought up to believe in Nazism. These beliefs included the rejection of Jews and other minority groups.

Humiliation

For Germany's 586,000 Jews, the impact of Hitler's **dictatorship** was immediate. Many were proud Germans who had fought for the "fatherland" in World War I. Most spoke German and thought of themselves as German. Moreover, some of Germany's finest poets, writers, scientists, and musicians had been Jewish. This made no

difference. In April, all Jews were made to wear the yellow **Star of David.** After this, they were picked on and humiliated in the streets. Their **gentile** friends were afraid to be seen out with them.

Boycott

The first planned action took place on April 1, 1933, when people were urged to **boycott** Jewish businesses. They were told that Jews were responsible for the economic crisis that had hit Germany after the war and that, while Germans had struggled to survive during the **depression** years, Jews had prospered. Jewish-owned shops were marked with the Star of David and slogans were painted on the windows and walls outside. Stormtroopers stood at shop doors and tried to discourage people from entering. This was followed by a law that resulted in Jewish teachers in German schools and universities and Jewish government workers being dismissed from their jobs.

The Nuremberg Laws, 1935

Each year, in Nuremberg, the Nazi Party held a huge rally. In 1935, this was the occasion chosen by Hitler to announce new laws against Jews and all people of Jewish descent. These became known as the Nuremberg Laws. These were very severe. Jews were not identified just as a religious community but as a race. Even people who were not of the faith but who had ancestors going back for four generations came within its terms. These harsh laws were supposed to help to purify the **Aryan** race by stopping mixed marriages. Couples who were of mixed Aryan and Jewish origin were forced to separate. Men and women were subjected to the indignity of having the proportions of their faces measured, as the Nazi regime tried to establish physical criteria to identify "Jewishness."

These Jewish businessmen were made to walk through the streets of Leipzig in 1935 carrying signs that said, "Don't buy from Jews; Shop in German businesses."

13

Persecution

Anti-Jewish posters were produced in many languages. This one was for Lithuania, part of Russia. The caption at the top says "The Jew—Your Eternal Enemy" and at the bottom, "Stalin and the Jews—One Evil Gang" (Stalin was the leader of communist Russia).

Aryanization

Hitler briefly halted his policies of persecution in 1936 when the Olympic Games were held in Berlin. Even so, German Jewish athletes were not allowed to compete and Hitler showed his contempt for those of what he defined as inferior races when he left the stadium to avoid presenting a gold medal to the African-American athlete Jesse Owens. In the three years that followed, before the outbreak of World War II in 1939, the policies of "aryanization" were stepped up.

Businesses owned by Jews were taken away and sold cheaply to those of "pure" **Aryan** blood. Jews in managerial positions lost their jobs; Jewish doctors were not allowed to treat non-Jews; Jewish lawyers were not allowed to practice. The identity cards carried by Jews carried a red letter "J" and those who did not have names that were easily recognizable as Jewish were given middle names—Israel for men; Sara for women—to be easily spotted by the police. Beatings and arrests became a common feature of life for the Jewish communities in all German towns. Communities that had once lived together without discrimination were now torn apart by hatred and suspicion.

Much of this was whipped up by the **Nazi propaganda** machine. Hitler, himself, frequently included attacks on the Jews in his speeches. Propaganda film showing sewer rats compared them to the Jews. Cartoons showing **stereotypical** images of Jewish men were all designed to emphasize their inferiority in the minds of Aryan Germans.

Kristallnacht—Night of Broken Glass

In November 1938, a young Jewish boy in Paris murdered a German official. This was used as the excuse for a carefully planned onslaught on Jewish communities throughout Germany. During the night of November 9 and through the next day, over 1,000 **synagogues** were burned, and around 7,000 Jewish shops were smashed and looted. Jewish cemeteries, hospitals, schools, and homes were also vandalized. The police watched and did nothing in spite of the fact that many Jews died. Some were beaten to death. The streets were littered with shattered glass from shop windows so the **pogrom** became known as the *Kristallnacht* or "Night of Broken Glass." The following day 30,000 Jewish men were arrested and deported to **concentration camps.** Their only "crime" was that they were Jewish.

These shop windows, like thousands of others belonging to Jewish shop owners, were smashed during the Kristallnacht.

The shrinking world of the Jewish child

All of this had a devastating effect on Jewish children. From April 25, 1933, when laws were passed to limit the number of Jewish students attending schools and universities, their world rapidly grew smaller and smaller. They lost friends and, in the case of children from mixed marriages, they also became separated from some members of their families after the Nuremberg Laws were passed. They were banned from visiting museums, public playing fields, and swimming pools. Those who still attended German schools were frequently humiliated in front of classmates who had once been their friends. After the *Kristallnacht,* they were expelled from schools and became totally segregated from the wider community.

Gypsies, homosexuals, and the handicapped

In their efforts to produce a pure Aryan race, the Nazis also persecuted others who were regarded as inferior. Between 1933 and 1935, laws were passed to reduce the numbers of these, firstly by compulsory sterilization programs. Children of African–German origin and the mentally or physically handicapped were surgically sterilized, often brutally, so that they could not have children. It is estimated that between 300,000 and 400,000 were subjected to the sterilization procedures. The same was true of Germany's 30,000 gypsies. They were banned from intermarrying. Many also ended their days in concentration camps as racial inferiors. Homosexuals were considered, along with trade unionists, Jehovah's Witnesses (a religious sect), and political opponents of the Nazis to be undesirable. Thousands experienced persecution and imprisonment in concentration camps.

Escape to Freedom

After the *Kristallnacht*, it is estimated that half of the German Jewish population and two-thirds of Austrian Jews left their homes, to escape persecution. It was a movement that the **Nazis** encouraged, having first taken most of their wealth and possessions from them. They emigrated to Palestine (modern-day Israel), the United States, Latin America, Canada, and China. This was not entirely successful for all of them. The United States, Canada, Britain, and France, where there were still economic problems and high unemployment, were reluctant to accept large numbers of **refugees,** and eventually closed their doors to them. No one at that point in time could have imagined what Hitler had in store for those who remained. Many who made their way to the Netherlands, France, and eastern Europe found themselves caught up again in the Nazi net after 1939, as Hitler overran these countries and extended his policy of **exterminating** the Jews.

The voyage of the *St. Louis*

On May 13, 1939, the *St. Louis* set sail from the port of Hamburg, Germany bound for Havana, Cuba carrying more than 900 Jewish refugees. Many had bought landing permits. They intended to wait in Cuba until they could enter the United States. At the time, the United States only allowed a certain number of immigrants each year. In the days before the ship's departure there had been demonstrations in Havana opposing Jewish immigration. When the ship arrived at the port on May 27, its passengers were refused entry. For the next five days, the ship sailed backwards and forwards, in intense heat, between Havana and Miami on the east coast of the United States while negotiations took place between the Cuban and U.S. immigration authorities and Jewish representatives. Efforts to persuade either country to accept all of the refugees failed. Finally, on June 6, the *St. Louis* headed back to Europe. Its passengers were frightened to return to Germany and pleaded with other European nations to give them a safe haven. By the time the ship docked at Antwerp in Belgium, Britain had agreed to receive 287 of the Jewish passengers, France 224, Belgium 214, and the Netherlands 181. The ship had been at sea for a month.

Julius Hermann, pictured below with his family, was a passenger on the St. Louis. He eventually reached France, where he was put in an **internment camp.** *In 1942, he was sent to Auschwitz, where he died.*

For many of these refugees the ordeal was not over. They had often been forced to spend or sell almost everything they had to buy their visas and tickets. Although they had been allowed to enter other countries, they were not necessarily welcomed. Often they were treated with suspicion, especially after the outbreak of World War II in 1939. After all, they were Germans—"enemy aliens." Some were eventually able to emigrate to the United States, especially if they already had family there. Many who settled in mainland Europe found themselves victims again of the Nazi **exterminators** as Germany occupied previously "safe" countries.

Doris Fogel lives today in Fort Wayne, Indiana. She was born in Berlin in 1935. Along with her mother, she was one of the 14,000 German and Austrian Jews who, in 1939, escaped from the Nazi terror and took refuge in Shanghai, China.

A photograph of Doris Fogel's class at her English-speaking Jewish school in Shanghai. Doris is third from the right, back row.

I was a refugee in May 1939 when I embarked with my mother on the ship Sharenhorst *from Rotterdam. We were outward bound for Shanghai, the only place in the world that required no entry visa. . . We had had to sell most of our possessions to obtain passage out of Germany. For a short period during 1939 our exile status was not yet quite apparent. We had valid German passports, even though a red stamped "J" was on the facing page of my mother's passport along with the red stamped "Sara" above her name, Edith Warschawski. Then Germany passed a new law that made our passports legally useless and removed citizenship from us. We became "stateless" persons.*

*I was four years old in 1939. My memories of Germany were non-existent and Shanghai became my home. I attended an English-speaking Jewish school. I made friends, played sports, was active in school activities. I was happy as were my school friends. None of us knew that we were poor nor did we feel deprived. . . We didn't know any better. We lived this **ghetto** life all through the war.*

*In 1941, the Japanese occupied Shanghai and, being **allies** of Nazi Germany, ordered that all Jewish refugees live in a poverty-stricken, filthy and unsanitary area of Shanghai called Hongkew. In this one square mile lived 20,000 refugees as prisoners of war. Life in Shanghai was primitive. My mother and I left Shanghai for the United States in April 1947.*

War and the Ghettos

Since coming to power, Hitler had built up Germany's fighting strength. From 1935, he began to extend the boundaries of Germany as part of his policy of creating **lebensraum.** This meant breaking the terms of the Treaty of Versailles, which were designed to stop Germany from becoming too powerful. Next, he took back the lands that Germany had lost. In 1936 he took the Rhineland. Then, in 1938–39, he absorbed Austria and Czechoslovakia into his **Reich.** At each stage, the **Allies** did nothing to stop him, refusing to believe that he intended total domination. Suddenly, on September 1, 1939, he launched a massive attack on Poland. This was a new tactic called *blitzkrieg*. Hitler used it again and again between 1939 and 1941 to occupy Denmark, Norway, Belgium, the Netherlands, France, Yugoslavia, and Greece. The English Channel helped to stop his westward expansion. In 1941, Hitler invaded the Soviet Union.

War offered the opportunity for the **Nazis** to extend their terrible plan to rid the world of Jews and "inferiors." No one at the time imagined that any power engaged in such a large-scale war could also have the resources and determination to carry out such a policy. More important, as Hitler overran European countries that had Jewish populations, he had the opportunity to realize his vision of **exterminating** the entire Jewish population.

This map shows the path of the Nazi invasion of Europe.

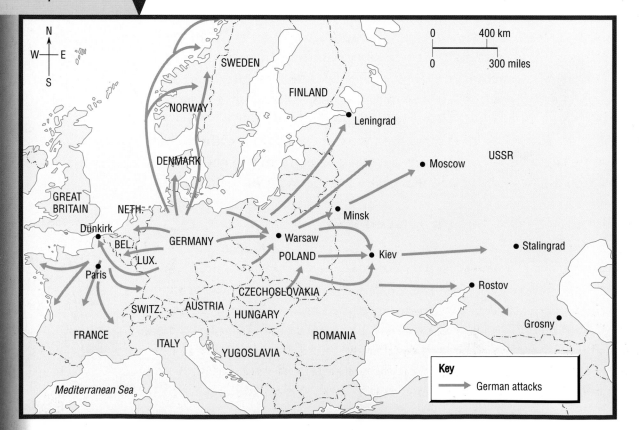

Into the ghettos

The Nazis adopted a policy known as *judenfrei*. As they occupied eastern European countries, they rounded up all Jews into sealed-off **ghetto** areas where they were effectively imprisoned. In the larger cities, these were walled off. Between 1939 and 1945, the Nazis created 356 ghettos in Poland, the Soviet Union, the **Baltic States,** Czechoslovakia, Romania, and Hungary.

Jews were forced to build an outer wall to enclose themselves within the Warsaw ghetto in Poland, 1941.

Life in the ghettos

Living conditions were terrible. The ghettos were unbearably overcrowded. The Warsaw ghetto in Poland, for example, held 400,000 people. There was no sanitation or clean water. Food was scarce and there was no heating. It is not surprising that in these filthy conditions, disease was rampant, killing many of the weakened population. Thousands also died of starvation.

The Nazis imposed the running of the ghetto onto a Jewish Council, which appointed its own police and was responsible for the day-to-day organization. It had to provide fit and healthy Jews over 16 years of age for forced labor. They had to work a 12-hour day. This often involved marching long distances, inadequately dressed for the weather. The work was hard—digging tunnels, hauling heavy materials, loading or unloading ships or aircraft, and building roads. They also worked in factories run by the Nazis. Large numbers died from the severity of the work. Others were deliberately killed. From 1942, many were deported from the ghettos to unknown destinations. Most of them were never seen again.

Terror in the Kovno ghetto, Lithuania

On October 28, 1941, the "Great Action" began in the Kovno ghetto. All of the inmates were assembled in the square. Some were sent to the right, some to the left. The next day, the 9,200 men, women, and children sent to the right were forced to undress and stand naked in the cold for several hours. Then the children were thrown into a deep ditch. The women were shot at the edge of the ditch so that they fell in, then the men. Many were buried alive. Events like this, public hangings, and other punishments meant inhabitants of all the ghettos lived in a permanent state of fear.

The Children of the Terezin Ghetto

Terezin, or Theresienstadt, is about 37 miles (60 km) from Prague in the present-day Czech Republic (formerly Czechoslovakia). It was built as a military fort in the 18th century. Between 1941 and 1945 it became a **ghetto** created by the **Nazis.** Jews were herded here from the whole of Czechoslovakia and beyond. Hitler claimed that it was a model city where Jews would be safe. He even showed it off to visitors from the Red Cross, an international charity. The city's bread, candy and cake stores, and gardens were specially created for the occasion. As in other ghettos, dirt, disease, cruelty, humiliation, hunger and fear were everyday features of life there.

Approximately 15,000 children passed through Terezin during these years. By the time they reached the ghetto, they had already been the victims of Nazi persecution. Their chances of survival depended very much on their ability to resist disease and to work. Infants, toddlers, and small children were especially vulnerable. At first, these children were cared for in kindergarten while their parents worked. But when the deportations began in 1942, the little ones were among the first to go.

Remarkable achievements

The children of Terezin, their parents, and grandparents are not forgotten. In the midst of all their hardships, these strong-willed inhabitants of the ghetto secretly held concerts and performed plays, determined to keep up their spirits. Musicians continued to play and composers composed. A children's operetta, *The Bumble Bee*, has survived. Meanwhile, the young ones painted, drew, wrote poetry, and kept diaries. A remarkable and moving collection of poems, writing, and pictures remain. They enable us to see through the eyes of these young people, the world that they inhabited during those terrible years.

Fear

Today the ghetto knows a different fear,
Close in its grip, Death wields an icy scythe.
An evil sickness spreads a terror in its wake,
The victims of its shadow weep and writhe.

Today a father's heartbeat tells his fright
And mothers bend their heads into their hands.
Now children choke and die with typhus here,
A bitter tax is taken from their bands.

My heart still beats inside my breast
While friends depart for other worlds.
Perhaps it's better—who can say?
Than watching this, to die today?

No, no, my God, we want to live!
Not watch our numbers melt away.
We want to have a better world,
We want to work—we must not die!

Eva Pickova (born May 15, 1929; died December 18, 1943, at Auschwitz)

The children were taught in secret. By drawing and painting, they were encouraged to develop their creativity as well as to express their feelings and emotions. The fantasy world that some of them entered, through their paintings, must have helped them to cope with the harsh and frightening reality of ghetto life. The older ones drew and wrote about their surroundings in the ghetto. Their work reflects the sadness of parting from friends and family. Some cry out for explanations of their persecution. Many yearn for freedom and a return to normality. For hundreds of these children, none of their hopes and dreams were realized. They never returned to their homes and families. Only their poems and paintings remain as a memorial, for by 1945, only 132 of the 15,000 had survived. A vast number had perished in the gas chambers of Auschwitz.

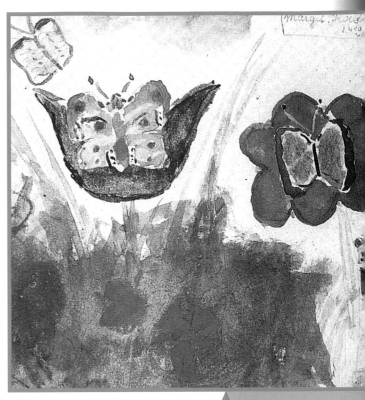

Margit Koretzova, age 11, was taken to the Terezin ghetto in 1942 where she painted this. She died in Auschwitz in 1944.

The saddest story

Perhaps the saddest story from the Terezin ghetto is that of the Bialystok children. In August 1943, the Nazis had entered the Bialystok ghetto in Poland with tanks and guns and wiped out the 40,000 Jews living there. The small group of surviving children were then taken, heavily guarded, to Terezin. On the day of their arrival, all the inmates were ordered indoors and forbidden to look out. The children were half-starved, dirty, and very frightened. When they were taken to the showers to be cleaned, they screamed, "Gas, gas!" No one at Terezin understood at the time what that meant. Doctors and nurses in the ghetto were taken away to care for the Bialystok children in a **quarantined** area.

On October 5, 1943, they all suddenly disappeared. At first, there were rumors that they had been taken to Switzerland to be handed over to the Red Cross in exchange for German prisoners. Investigations after the War have proved that, while the children had been at the center of some kind of deal, the plans had all come to a tragic end. Instead of traveling to Switzerland, they were transported to Auschwitz and sent to the gas chambers immediately on their arrival, together with the doctors and nurses who cared for them. One of the nurses who accompanied them was Hana Greenfield's mother.

The Camps

The first camps were constructed in Germany and used by the **Nazi** regime to hold anyone that they wanted to remove from society. The first **concentration camp,** Dachau, was built in March 1933 when Hitler came to power. Others soon followed. They housed a variety of people, including political opponents such as **communists** and members of opposition parties in the former democratic government, and Protestant and Catholic clergy who criticized him. Once Hitler started to attack those he believed to be inferior, the occupants of his camps included Jews, gypsies, homosexuals, and Jehovah's Witnesses (a religious sect). Anyone else who was careless enough to make critical remarks in the hearing of Hitler's secret police, the Gestapo, or their spies could also find themselves behind the barbed wire of the camps.

This map shows the location of concentration and death camps across Europe.

By 1942, there were camps for a variety of purposes. As well as the concentration camps, there were forced labor camps and even more horrific, the **death camps.** As the Nazis overran Europe after 1939, the network of camps was extended into all occupied countries.

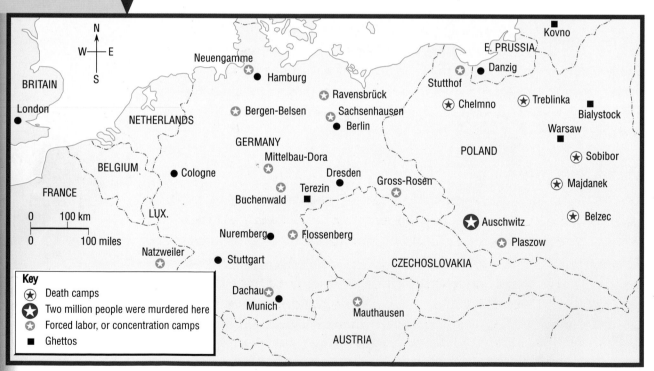

A vicious routine

By 1942, there were an estimated 100,000 prisoners in the camps. By January 1945, it is claimed that there were around 700,000. But between 1933 and 1945, thousands more had passed through the camps and thousands had perished. The inmates of concentration and forced labor camps were either starved or worked to death. They could barely exist in the cramped and dirty conditions. Hundreds died in frequent epidemics of typhus as a result of the lack of sanitation. The daily routine included endless roll calls (*appells*). This could mean standing for several hours, often in wet or icy conditions. Severe beatings and random executions were also part of this routine as was the forced labor. Women were especially vulnerable to abuse.

This painting by a German girl from Neugraben camp near Hamburg, Germany, shows a guard punishing her friend.

Medical experiments

At Dachau, selected prisoners were used for medical experimentation. These involved a series of experiments to test the reaction of the body to various conditions such as high altitude, freezing temperatures, and atmospheric pressure. Others were associated with diseases and conditions such as hepatitis, tuberculosis, and malaria. The pain and suffering caused to these human "guinea pigs" must have been intense and excruciating.

Mengele's children

Josef Mengele became notorious for his cruel experiments using children at Auschwitz. He was particularly obsessed with twins and inherited characteristics. He wanted to find the formula that would ensure that **Aryan** women gave birth to blonde, blue-eyed children. As Jewish families entered the death camp, twins were wrenched from their mothers. Sometimes, parents gave up their twins hoping they might be saved, ignorant of what was planned for them. Mothers were occasionally allowed to go with their children to look after them. They were tattooed with a number and taken to a special barracks. Mengele gained the children's trust by giving them candy and often playing with them. Some of them actually called him "Uncle Mengele." Their affection did not stop him from carrying out horrific surgical experiments on them without anaesthetic. The children were maimed, paralyzed, and hundreds of them died as a result. Many were deliberately killed for post-mortem ("after death") experiments. Of all the horrors of the camps, this was one of the worst.

Genocide

Forced labor

Just as the **ghettos** provided forced labor for factories and work sites, so able-bodied political prisoners, gypsies, and Jews in the camps were selected for harsh and grueling work. As the war continued, Germany was put under increasing pressure. This was especially true as the fighting in Russia went badly for Hitler. The war effort had to be stepped up. Most of the major German firms relied on slave labor and camps were established near large industrial plants. The workers were not treated as though they had any value. When they literally dropped dead from exhaustion or were casually shot because they had become weak and, therefore, "worthless," there were other Jews or gypsies to replace them.

The euthanasia program

While the major world powers were concentrating on fighting World War II, Hitler was working behind the scenes to purify the **Aryan** race and, particularly, to fulfill his mission of freeing the world from Jews. His plans began in earnest from 1940. In various institutions in Germany and elsewhere, such as the Steinhof clinic in Vienna, the **Nazis** planned and carried out the murder of hundreds of mentally and physically handicapped children. Parents were encouraged to send their children to these clinics believing that they would receive the best care. Instead, they were systematically murdered either by starvation and neglect, lethal injection, or by specially appointed killing units. These were basically vans that carried handicapped children to an appointed place where, as the vehicle stood, carbon monoxide was deliberately pumped into it, suffocating the children. Their bodies were then burned in huge ovens called crematoria. Many of the guards were sickened by what they were being made to do.

Between 1940 and 1945, more than 200,000 handicapped people, mainly children, were murdered. The euthanasia program was the first stage of

This drawing, by Dina Gottlieb, is called "Returning from Work." It captures the mood of the starving and exhausted women. On their return to the camp from a day's hard labor in Hamburg, they were given only a chunk of bread and a bowl of thin, watery soup.

Hitler's master plan. It offered the opportunity to try out a carefully planned process of mass murder. This project provided experience for those Nazi officers who were to mastermind the total **extermination** of the Jews, gypsies, and other "undesirables." It was the training ground for the gas chambers and crematoria of the **death camps.**

This photograph of a group of children was taken shortly before they were killed by a mobile killing squad in the former Soviet Union.

Massacre at Babi Yar

On the outskirts of Kiev, the capital city of Ukraine, is a place called Babi Yar. Today, it is in a suburb of the growing capital of an independent country. In 1941, Ukraine was still part of the Soviet Union and Babi Yar was merely a deep ravine in open countryside. In June, 1941, Hitler invaded the Soviet Union and occupied much of Ukraine. Between September 29 and 30, 1941, 33,000 Ukrainian Jews were herded from the city center, where they lived, to the Babi Yar ravine. The road out of the city became littered with bodies of those shot on the way. When they arrived, they were ordered to hand over all their possessions and to remove their clothing. They were forced to stand and watch as row upon row of men, women, and children were lined up along the edge of the ravine and systematically shot so that their bodies fell into its depths. In the two years that followed, thousands of gypsies and Soviet prisoners of war were also executed there.

The *Einsatzgruppen*

The executions at Babi Yar were carried out by specially appointed, mobile killing squads, called the *Einsatzgruppen*. These mass killing units, operated all over eastern Europe and were made up of local recruits in Ukraine and Lithuania, where **anti-Semitism** was strong. Hundreds of thousands died in the same way as the people at Babi Yar all over eastern Europe and the Soviet Union. This was one of the ways that Hitler planned the final phase of his racist policy. It was one aspect of his so-called "final solution."

The "Final Solution"

The Wannsee Conference, 1942

On January 20, 1942, Hitler met with his senior officials at Wannsee, on the outskirts of Berlin. There they adopted, as official policy, Hitler's plan to **exterminate** eleven million Jews. These included Jews in countries that were not at that time occupied by the **Nazis,** such as Britain. It is hard to believe, if you visit this pretty lakeland area today, that such an evil plan could have been devised there. Outwardly, the plan seemed to be to round up all the Jews, transport them to the east and literally work them to death. Although there was reference to the "final solution," **genocide** was not openly spoken of. However, immediately after the meeting, preparations were made to install poison-gas chambers in what came to be known as extermination or **death camps.** The administration of the "final solution" of the Jewish "problem" was to be the responsibility of Adolf Eichmann.

The gateway to Auschwitz. The words mean "Work makes you free." As new prisoners arrived, they were greeted with music to make them think they were entering a happy place.

Auschwitz

There were six death camps —Belzec, Sobibor, Treblinka, Chelmo, Majdanek, and Auschwitz-Birkenau. (See map on page 22.) All were in semi-rural locations but close to a railway line. All were responsible for gassing hundreds of thousands of Jews in the gas vans or chambers. However, Auschwitz-Birkenau, in Poland, became the most notorious. Throughout the war, this served as a **concentration,** forced labor, and then death camp. In September 1941, 850 Polish prisoners and Soviet prisoners of war (POWs) were used to try out the gassing procedures. Between 1941 and 1945, 1.25 million men, women, and children died there. These included gypsies and Soviet POWs, but nine in every ten were Jews. Between May and July 1944, the largest single group of **deportees,** 437,402 Hungarian Jews, arrived at Auschwitz in 48 trains and were gassed.

Deportees arrived in cattle trucks from the **ghettos** and camps all over occupied Europe. The conditions on the trains were horrific. When they were unloaded, many had died from suffocation or lack of food and water. Guards with whips, guns, and dogs greeted them. Men were separated from women and children. Some were selected for slave labor and the rest for immediate execution. Hana Greenfield (see page 5) escaped the gas chambers when she arrived at Auschwitz because she was selected for work. She survived.

The dead were loaded into carts, wheeled to these ovens at Auschwitz, and burned.

Death in the gas chambers

Those who were to die were marched away. They were told to undress for a shower after their long journey and then driven into what appeared to be huge shower rooms. When the showers were turned on, however, it was not water that came out but deadly gas, either carbon monoxide or Zyklon B. Other Jewish prisoners were forced to take the bodies from the gas chambers to the ovens where they were burned. These prisoners had to remain silent as they watched their fellow Jews going to their deaths.

Back in the ghettos, the daily transportations of large numbers of inmates caused concern, but people were ignorant of the fate that was to await them when they reached their destination. For those who remained and survived, they were not to discover the terrible truth until after the war ended and the camps were **liberated.**

A changed man

Large numbers of small children were transported to the death camps. They were too young to work so, when they arrived, if they were not selected for medical experimentation, they were immediately gassed. At this time, a successful businessman and Nazi supporter in the Polish town of Kraków watched each day as the small ghetto children were marched along to their kindergarten, singing as they went. There they stayed all day while their parents worked on forced labor gangs and then returned to them in the evening. One evening, as he watched, the children did not return. He was shocked as he realized what must have happened to them. It changed this man's life forever. His name was Oskar Schindler.

The Will to Resist

Photographs and film footage of the Holocaust sometimes present us with striking images of lines of the victims standing quietly and passively waiting to die. On the one hand, they suggest an admirable dignity in the face of atrocity. They can also give the impression of a meek and submissive people who have abandoned hope and lost the will to live. But we must not imagine that the inmates of the **ghettos** and camps lost their sense of self-respect or their will to survive. On the contrary, in the ghettos and the camps there was defiance and resistance which showed themselves in a variety of ways.

Organization and culture in the ghettos

One admirable form of passive resistance was the determination of Jewish communities in the ghettos to maintain some quality of life for themselves and their families in spite of the squalor in which they were condemned to live. The Jewish Council in each ghetto endeavored to manage the day-to-day life of the ghetto so that the shortage of living space and of food, and the outbreaks of disease were dealt with in an orderly and organized way. They also ensured that the religious life of the people was maintained and that their talents and abilities continued to be developed for the benefit of all.

Much of this had to be done in secret, away from the destructive eyes of **Nazi** guards. Children continued to be educated and encouraged to express themselves in art, poetry, and writing. Music flourished, especially in the ghetto of Terezin. The inmates were entertained by quartets, an orchestra, a chamber music ensemble, and a jazz band. It is amazing that, with the threat of death hanging over him, Viktor Ullmann composed twenty pieces of music at Terezin. It is a strange irony that, while treating the Jews so abominably, their Nazi captors were happy to be entertained by them.

This is an extract from the diary of Ilya Gerber, an inmate of the Kovno ghetto, for December 28, 1942. It reads, "Musical circles are working at 120 percent, concerts are organized, there are rehearsals, people sing, they play, they blow, and they tickle their instruments. . ."

The Kovno ghetto's secret history

In 1941, when Hitler invaded, Lithuania was part of the Soviet Union. It was clearly his intention that the Jews in Lithuania would be quickly **exterminated** by the *Einsatzgruppen*. By February 1942, over 136,421 had been killed, many of them with extreme brutality. Those that survived the killing squads were confined to ghettos in the large towns and provided slave labor for the Nazis. Following the murder of 9,200 Jewish inhabitants of the Kovno ghetto in Lithuania in October 1941, the leader of the Jewish Council, Dr. Elkhanan Elkes, urged his people to show their defiance of the Nazis by building up an archive of material that would eventually tell the world what had been done there. The inmates were encouraged to keep diaries. Artists painted pictures and a good photographer kept a photographic record. As long as possible, all of this was hidden away. When the ghetto was finally destroyed in 1944, much of the material collected was also destroyed. But some had been well buried and so survived as a unique record of what the Nazis had done there.

Jewish resistance fighters

Some Jews managed to escape from the ghettos and camps. Some literally made a dash for woodland areas during mass killings in eastern Europe. As many as 20,000 lived and fought in the forests there. Jews also joined in resistance activities in France

Here is a photograph of Jewish resistance fighters in Lithuania, around 1943.

(where a "Jewish Army" was formed), Italy, and Belgium. They became involved in acts of sabotage, such as blowing up railway lines. Others used their skills to forge documents and identity cards to help the **Allied** war effort. Life was hard for them because, as Jews, they could not always rely on the support of the local people even though they had a common cause. Sometimes they were betrayed to the Gestapo (Nazi secret police).

Resistance in the Warsaw Ghetto, 1942

There were resistance groups within most of the camps and **ghettos.** This resulted in uprisings at Treblinka and Sobibor in 1943 and at Auschwitz in 1944. The most well-known act of resistance and defiance was the revolt in the Warsaw ghetto.

Mordecai Anielewicz and the *ZOB*

By the summer of 1942, 300,000 Jews from Warsaw had been deported to the **death camp** of Treblinka. However, news got back to those living in the Warsaw ghetto about what was happening to the **deportees** when they reached their destination. As a result, the young inhabitants of the ghetto, led by Mordecai Anielewicz, joined together to organize resistance to deportation.

Anielewicz already had a reputation as a revolutionary. He believed that, in the face of persecution, the Jews should take up arms to defend themselves. He was very active in the ghetto, encouraging and organizing educational and cultural activities. He also helped to produce a newspaper called *Neged Hazerem* ("Against the Stream"). The result was the setting up of the Jewish Combat Organization (*Zydowska Organizacja Bojowa* or *ZOB*). With the help of another resistance fighter, Itzhak Zuckerman, the *ZOB* obtained guns and hand grenades so that when the **Nazis** tried to organize a shipment of Jews from the ghetto on January 18, 1943, they were met with armed resistance. The Germans withdrew after about fifty soldiers were killed in the street fighting that went on for the next four days.

This memorial to Janusz Korczak is at the Yad Vashem National Memorial of the Holocaust in Jerusalem, Israel.

Janusz Korczak

Janusz Korczak was a great educator who had been the head of an orphanage in Warsaw since 1912. He accompanied his orphans to the death chambers of Treblinka in August 1942 and is remembered for his love and care for the children.

A birthday gift for Hitler

This "stand off" lasted until April 19, the first day of the **Feast of the Passover** in the Jewish calendar. The next day was Hitler's birthday. It was planned to retake the ghetto to celebrate his birthday. The Nazis assembled 20,000 heavily armed troops and tanks.

While the remaining Jews in the ghetto hid in the underground bunkers that they had built, Anielewicz and a 1,500-strong Jewish resistance army fought to stop the Germans from entering the ghetto. Casualties were high. The Germans used flame throwers, gas, and dogs. Thousands were burned alive in the ghetto, many of them leaping from high buildings. But the ZOB still managed to hold out in their bunker until May 8 when many of the young fighters, including Anielewicz, committed suicide rather than be captured. The battle ended on May 16. The remaining Jews were deported and the ghetto was totally demolished. The last Nazi action against this incredible effort to resist was the destruction of the Great **Synagogue** of Warsaw. The commanding officer, Major General Jürgen Stoop, reported to Berlin, "The Warsaw ghetto is no more."

This photograph shows German soldiers rounding up Jews in the Warsaw ghetto after the 1943 uprising.

The diary of Abraham Lewin

Parts of this remarkable diary were found hidden in 1946 and 1950. They cover the period from March 1942 until January 1943. They capture the atmosphere of fear and apprehension during the last days of the Warsaw ghetto, when the people were desperate and starving.

Wednesday, July 22, 1942
. . . The expulsion is supposed to begin today from the hostels for the homeless and from the prisons . . . Beggar children are being rounded up into wagons. I am thinking about my aged mother. It would be better to put her to sleep than to hand her over to those murderers . . .

Sunday, August 16, 1942
Today is the 26th day of the "action," which is continuing with all its atrocities and animal savagery, a slaughter the like of which human history has not seen. . . . People . . . have told of women who were seized yesterday who were freed if they sacrificed their children . . . they were separated from their children aged 3 to 12 to 14. Any woman carrying a child or with a child next to her was not freed. The Germans' lust for Jewish blood knows no bounds, it is a bottomless pit. Future generations will not believe it . . .

"Rescuers"

Yad Vashem is the national memorial museum in Jerusalem, Israel to the victims of the Holocaust. Besides commemorating those who died, Yad Vashem honors those **gentiles** from all over occupied Europe who risked their lives to help their Jewish countrymen and women. Currently, these people number 17,433. Many of their efforts only came to be known after the war ended. Now they are known there as "The Righteous among the Nations." Names are still being added to the list as more and more survivors tell of their experiences and describe what they owe to those who hid or rescued them. These personal testimonies frequently acknowledge small acts of kindness from unknown and often unseen helpers. Those who, from behind curtained windows, threw bread to starving forced labor gangs, for example, or took the opportunity in a passing moment to show kindness.

Hana's boots

In the winter of 1944, Hana Greenfield (see page 5) was in a forced labor gang working in Hamburg. It was icy cold, yet the women and girls were forced to work outside in their striped prison clothing, without underwear, hats, gloves, or adequate footwear. One day, desperately cold, she escaped briefly and knocked on the door of a house where she hoped the people would take pity on her and let her in to warm herself.

The woman let her in and gave her a bowl of hot soup which she ate hurriedly so that she would not be missed by the guards. As she left, the woman told her to call again when she could. She did so two days later. This time, besides the soup, there was a pair of old shoes that the man of the house had repaired for her. They were so big that they had to be stuffed with newspaper, but they kept her feet warm and dry. Hana never saw the couple again. At the end of her story, she says this: *I never learned the names of those good people nor their address, but for the rest of the winter I blessed them. . . These were righteous gentiles. . . In the difficult days I lived through in Hamburg during the war, I found two good people who restored my faith in humanity. . .*

This card was produced in Holland to raise money to help Jewish people in hiding. The quotation says, "Never forget to be hospitable, for by hospitality some have entertained angels unawares."

Vergeet de herbergzaamheid niet!

HEBR. 13:2

Righteous gentiles

All of the people honored by Yad Vashem have their own stories to tell. Many of them were ordinary people who gave homes to small children to save them from deportation or who tried to save whole families from being sent to the **death camps** by hiding them. The story of Anne Frank is now well known because of her famous diary. A large number of Dutch people were active in saving Jews even though the Netherlands lost 80–90 percent of its Jewish population.

Community action

There are also examples of national and local community action to protect the Jewish population. The Danish government resisted the demands of the **Nazi** regime to give up its Jewish population. From September 1943, when news arrived of the secret intention to deport Danish Jews, a nationwide operation was undertaken to smuggle them to Sweden, a **neutral**

This photograph includes some of the many children who survived the Holocaust because they were cared for by the Christian people of Le Chambord-sur-Lignon, southern France (1942).

country. Jews were hidden in churches, hospitals, and private homes until they could be ferried in fishing boats across to Sweden. Of the 500 who were **deported** to the Terezin **ghetto,** all but 51 survived thanks to the continued interest that the Danish government took in their welfare.

In Bulgaria, the government saved its 48,000 native-born Jews by agreeing to put them into **internment camps,** but refusing to allow them to be transported from Bulgaria. Meanwhile in Poland, in the years after the Warsaw ghetto had been set up, approximately 20,000 Polish Jews survived because they were hidden by their Christian neighbors. The director of the Warsaw Zoo, Jan Zabinski, sheltered Jews in his zoo!

In France, one of many outstanding examples of courage is that of the community of the small village of Le Chambord-sur-Lignon where the inhabitants saved 5,000 Jews between 1941 and 1944 by hiding them in their homes, churches, and convents.

Heroes of the Holocaust

Schindler's List

Along the Avenue of the Righteous Among the Nations at Yad Vashem in Jerusalem are trees dedicated to those individuals who were prepared to risk their lives to save Jewish people. Among these is one dedicated to Oskar Schindler. Schindler's efforts have become widely known since Steven Spielberg made them the subject of his film, "Schindler's List." In the early years of the war, Schindler had done well from the **Nazi** regime. He had been rewarded for his support of the Nazis by being given an enamel factory in Kraków, Poland that had been taken from its Jewish owners. Schindler intended to make a fortune making pots and pans for the German army using Jewish slave labor from the Kraków **ghetto.** He seemed to flourish until that fateful day when the children from the ghetto did not return from the kindergarten. They had been **deported** to the gas chambers of Auschwitz.

From that moment, Schindler could no longer bear to see the brutal treatment of Jews, or to tolerate mass murder and do nothing. He was able to use his influence with the Nazis to secure a workforce of Jews. He was allowed to keep them in a camp near his factory where he tried to ensure that they were well treated. When he moved his business to Brunnlitz, he was allowed to take his workforce with him. When the war ended, Schindler had to escape as he was identified as a Nazi. Although he became a fugitive, he had rescued 1,200 Jews, considerably more than any other German rescuer.

Raoul Wallenberg

Some of the **diplomats** from **neutral** countries, who found themselves in embassies in occupied countries, used their positions to help persecuted people, especially Jews. Yad Vashem currently honors eighteen such people from European countries, China, and Japan.

Oskar Schindler was a hero made famous by the U.S. film director Steven Spielberg.

Of these, the exploits of Raoul Wallenberg are significant. He was a Swedish diplomat working in Budapest, Hungary. In 1944, he issued Swedish passports to Hungarian Jews to protect them from being deported to the **death camps.** He even chased after deportation convoys to rescue Jews on the basis that they were Swedish passport holders. He identified a number of "safe houses" in which rescued Jews could hide. He saved tens of thousands of people. In 1945, Wallenberg disappeared when Budapest was **liberated** by the army of the Soviet Union. It was later alleged that this man, who did so much for others, died in a Soviet prison in 1947.

Frank Foley

Foley was a British agent working for **MI6.** In the early years of the Hitler regime, he worked in the British Passport Control Office in Berlin. This was his cover for his spying activities. Foley witnessed the dreadful events of *Kristallnacht* and the effects of Hitler's anti-Jewish policies. He used his position to obtain and issue false visas and other documentation needed to enable German Jews to leave the country and, in many cases, to go to Palestine. It is estimated that, at great risk to himself, he saved the lives of about 10,000 Jews.

Raoul Wallenberg used his position of diplomatic authority to help Hungarian Jews.

These "righteous **gentiles,**" however, are a small proportion of the people who watched and did nothing to help persecuted Jews. Undoubtedly, many were too frightened to help. The penalties for doing so were severe. Sadly, **anti-Semitism** was so strong in some parts of occupied Europe that there were those who would not lift a finger to help a Jew. Others were even happy to help the Nazis with their dreadful work. The Nazis kept their deeds so well hidden that people in many parts of Europe only discovered the truth in the closing years of the war. By 1944, the U.S. government had been persuaded to set up the War Refugee Board to help rescue Jews. Approximately 200,000 were saved. In the meantime, the major powers of Europe believed that their energies were best devoted to the defeat of Hitler and to ridding the world of Nazism.

The Beginning of the End

D-Day, 1944

In June 1944, the forces of Britain, the United States, and Canada landed on the beaches of Normandy. The **liberation** of Europe had begun. As the **Allied forces** pushed the German army eastwards, the forces of the Soviet Union moved on Germany from the east. In spite of fierce resistance, it was clear that the days of **Nazi** Germany were numbered. This realization threw the Nazis into panic. By the early months of 1945, the liberating armies were advancing on the camps, especially in Poland and the **Baltic States.** They hurriedly tried to hide the evil acts that had been committed there. The dead and their belongings were hastily burned. The prisoners were moved.

Death marches

This must have been one of the most terrifying times for the surviving inmates of the camps. At Stutthof on the Baltic coast, hundreds were forced into barges and pushed out to sea where they drowned. Vast numbers were forced to march hundreds of miles (kilometers) away from the advancing armies. The old and those too sick and weak to walk were shot and left by the roadside. The biggest exodus of prisoners was from Auschwitz. One survivor described how her shoes froze to her feet as she walked. Another recounted how prisoners at Bergen–Belsen were loaded into railway carriages and left for two weeks among the sick and dead. By this time a large number were suffering from typhus. She also had meningitis. All were emaciated because of hunger and sickness. At Bergen–Belsen, where typhus and dysentery had reached epidemic proportions, conditions were filthy. Survivors, describing these conditions, talk of how they picked the lice from their bodies.

The piles of victims' belongings found at Auschwitz were chilling evidence of the number of lives that had been destroyed there.

Liberation!

In April and May of 1945, Allied forces entered the camps. Their reaction was one of shock, horror, and fury. What, for many of the war years, had been rumors and stories now became harsh reality. At Auschwitz, the gas chambers and crematoria had been blown up by the retreating Germans, but there was plenty of evidence of the enormity of the crime that had been committed there. For example, there were piles of personal belongings, shoes, glasses, suitcases (from countries all over Europe), and clothing of adults and children. Most sinister of all were the millions of Zyklon B gas canisters that had been used to murder at least one and a half million Jews and gypsies, and maybe many thousands more.

In some of the camps, German prison guards were shot as they tried to escape. In Germany, at Bergen-Belsen, the British forces who liberated the camp made the guards, male and female, load the bodies of the dead onto trucks and clean up those suffering from typhus and dysentery. Many of them subsequently caught these diseases themselves and died. Local people were taken to see the massive human tragedy that had been acted out there. The shocked German citizens of the town of Weimar were taken to Buchenwald **concentration camp,** to be shown the atrocities that had taken place almost on their doorsteps.

After liberation, the people of Weimar were shown Buchenwald concentration camp.

In the Far East

Meanwhile, for Doris Fogel in the Hongkew **ghetto** in Shanghai (see page 17), the end of the war against Japan was the most frightening time. The Japanese had deliberately stacked their remaining ammunition around the outside of the ghetto area. When the U.S. air force began to bomb Shanghai many of the inhabitants of the ghetto were killed.

For thousands, World War II had ended in 1945. But for those Jews liberated from the camps, it was only the beginning of the end of their troubles.

The Survivors

When World War II ended, the problem of returning **refugees** to their homes had to be solved. It was a slow and difficult task. Many different groups of people had moved far from their homes because of the fighting and destruction of their towns and villages. For the survivors of the Holocaust, it was almost impossible to resolve. As the survivors emerged from the camps, grateful for their freedom but sick and weak, their reactions were those of lost and bewildered souls. At first, they had no way of knowing how many members of their families had survived. The communities in which they had lived had been destroyed. They had been systematically demoralized and humiliated as well as punished and abused. Some survivors describe their total loss of self-esteem.

Ignorance and anti-Semitism

Even if survivors wanted to talk about their experiences in the **ghettos** and camps, there seemed to be no one in those post-war days who wanted to hear. For example, in January 1946, Hana Greenfield (see page 5) arrived in England where her uncle had lived throughout the war. She was told not to upset the family by telling them what had happened to her. She, however, desperately needed to do so in order to be able to rebuild her life. Other survivors clearly believed that what had happened to them was something of which they should be ashamed. Certainly, for those who stayed in Europe, their suffering was not over.

Nazi prisoners were guarded by U.S. soldiers as they awaited trial for war crimes held at Nuremberg, in northern Germany.

The terrible things that had happened to the Jews during the war did nothing to remove **anti-Semitism.** In some parts of Europe, Hitler had been able to count on the support of many sections of the population who hated Jews. After the war, Jews returning from the camps received a hostile reception. Anti-Jewish riots broke out in Poland, for example. In 1946, a group of 150 Polish Jews returning to their native town of Kielce to reclaim their belongings were attacked. Forty of them were killed and fifty were injured.

Perhaps the extent of anti-Semitism can be appreciated by the fact that many of the Christian population who had sheltered Jews found themselves the victims of reprisals for their acts of kindness after the war. Some of them eventually emigrated to Israel.

The Nuremberg Trials, 1945–1946

At least there was some punishment for the crimes that had been committed. Those responsible for the atrocities of the war years had to answer for their actions. By the time the Soviet forces reached Berlin, Hitler had committed suicide. Some of the more notorious Nazis, including Adolf Eichmann, had escaped. Those that remained were finally brought to trial, at Nuremberg. To some of the Nazis who stood trial, the dreadful orders they had issued had merely been words on pieces of paper. They never saw them carried out. They remained arrogant and showed no regret for what they had done. Others seem to have been able to convince themselves, or to have been brainwashed into believing, that they were not dealing with human beings when they drove thousands into the gas chambers with whips and dogs.

Judges from Britain, the United States, and the Soviet Union heard the evidence and passed judgment. In the end, twelve leading Nazis were sentenced to death; others received prison sentences. Further war crimes' trials were held all over Europe. These were mainly of camp guards, local police officers who had collaborated, members of the mobile killing squads, and doctors who took part in the medical experiments. The majority received prison sentences. Many more escaped justice.

*Adolf Eichmann, who had organized the **deportation** of Jews to the gas chambers, finally answered for his crimes in Jerusalem in 1962. He was found guilty of **genocide** and hanged.*

Simon Wiesenthal

Wiesenthal was a survivor of the Holocaust. His wife also survived. Eighty-nine members of their two families perished. Wiesenthal devoted himself to seeking out war criminals and bringing them to justice. Helped by the Israeli Secret Service, he rooted out Eichmann from his hiding place in Argentina in 1960. In the years that followed, he brought about the arrest and trial of 1,000 Nazis. In 1967, he was also responsible for finding Fritz Stangl, the former commandant of the **death camps** of Treblinka and Sobibor.

In Search of a Homeland

Lonely and without the support of families and friends, survivors had to face the challenge of rebuilding their lives. Young people, like Hana Greenfield (see page 5), had spent their teenage years in captivity. They had been deprived of education. They had lost the people they loved most in the world. They had nowhere to go. Ironically, many of them found themselves in displaced persons' camps set up by the **Allies** in western Europe on the sites of former **Nazi concentration camps.** The United States, Britain, and many European countries still had immigration policies in place, so for those who wanted to begin a new life in a new land, there was a waiting period. Eventually, survivors were able to immigrate to the United States, South America, South Africa, and Australia. Doris Fogel (see page 17) left Shanghai with her mother in April 1947 on board a converted U.S. troop ship, the SS *General Gordon,* and arrived in San Francisco, California on May 16. Hana Greenfield went to live in Israel, the new homeland for the Jews.

The Jewish refugee ship Pan York *docks at Haifa, in the newly established state of Israel, July 1948.*

A Jewish homeland

The idea that the Jews should have a homeland, Palestine, gained force at the end of the 19th century. Here they would be finally free from persecution. The plan was that of an Austrian Jew named Theodore Herzl. He started an organization called the Zionists to press for this to happen. After World War I, Palestine became a British protectorate (a country that is officially protected and partly controlled by another country). Herzl had already persuaded the British government to support his plan. But it was not quite as simple as that. Arab peoples now lived in Palestine. What would happen to them if it was handed over to Jews? During World War I (1914–1918), Britain needed the help of the Arabs to fight the Turks. The Arab leaders were promised that they would not lose Palestine and that Jewish immigration would be controlled. The British government of the day had obviously got itself into difficulties. It had made promises to two groups who would not even sit down together to discuss the situation.

In 1939, the British government said that only 77,000 Jews would be allowed to enter Palestine. It was hoped that this would pacify the Arabs. This was, of course, before the Holocaust. In 1946, a ship full of Jewish immigrants tried to enter Palestine illegally. They were turned back and sent to Cyprus where they were put in a British-run **internment camp.** The action of the British towards these survivors of Nazi persecution was severely criticized.

Doris Fogel (right) with two of her friends from her days in Shanghai. Of the original 21 members of her class, 17 have been traced, despite being scattered throughout the United States and other parts of the world. This photograph was taken in 1999 when they held a reunion in Philadelphia, Pennsylvania.

The United Nations tried to resolve the conflict in 1947 by dividing Palestine between Jews and Arabs. On May 14, 1948, David Ben-Gurion, the first prime minister, announced the creation of the state of Israel. For the first time in almost two thousand years, the Jews had their own homeland. However, this was achieved at great cost to the Palestinian Arabs who were denied their land and condemned to live in **refugee** camps. Hence, the establishment of the state of Israel opened up a new era of controversy and international conflict. The violent hatred that came to exist between Jews and Arabs showed itself in open warfare and terrorist activity during the last decades of the 20th century and the beginning of the next.

New beginnings

In 1962, the trial of Adolf Eichmann was a turning point in the lives of the Holocaust survivors. So many were called to provide evidence of the horrors that they had witnessed and experienced that they finally had the opportunity to speak out, to be heard, and in a sense free themselves of the nightmare that they had lived through. At last they could move on. In their new homes in Europe, the United States, Israel or wherever they settled, they married, had families, and went on to lead full and productive lives. In their amazing ability to rescue new hope and enthusiasm for life from the depths of despair, they are an example and inspiration to us all.

Preserving the Past

The Holocaust was the most appalling crime against humanity of the 20th century, if not of the history of humankind. It must never be forgotten. In addition to the six million Jews who lost their lives, an estimated five and a half million others also died. These included gypsies, Jehovah's Witnesses (a religious sect), homosexuals, critics of the **Nazi** government, and the mentally and physically handicapped. In addition, there were thousands and thousands who survived but who had been exposed to such horrific cruelty that it is impossible to imagine.

Remembrance

In Jerusalem, the impressive memorials at Yad Vasem honor those Jews who died in the Holocaust and those known and unknown **gentiles** who helped thousands to survive. Of the 23 memorials, perhaps the most moving is that to the one and a half million children who died. This is in an underground cavern where reflected candlelight produces the impression of millions of stars representing the lost life of each child. The memorial was donated by the parents of Uziel Spiegel, who was murdered in Auschwitz when he was two and a half years old.

In the cities of Europe, where Jewish communities once thrived, impressive memorials honor those who perished. An important part of remembrance is also the collection of evidence of the Holocaust to ensure that every painful detail is not forgotten. The United States Holocaust Memorial Museum in Washington, D.C. is a rich source of knowledge and of survivors' testimonies. More recently, a massive project has been undertaken by the Shoah Visual History Foundation, inspired by film director Steven Spielberg. This project has recorded the memories of the survivors for posterity and made them available to all via the Internet, ensuring that the Holocaust will never be forgotten.

This impressive willow tree made of stainless steel commemorates the Hungarian Jews who died in the Holocaust. Each silver leaf is a family memorial. It stands in the grounds of the Dohany **Synagogue,** *Budapest, in a memorial garden. Adolf Eichmann had set up his headquarters in this synagogue to organize* **deportations** *to the* **death camps.**

The lessons of the past

The story of the Holocaust is one of pain and suffering on a massive scale. Some say that it should be allowed to move into the past or that it is unhealthy to relive its agony. This cannot be true. It is only by facing up to what happened that we can hope to learn from it and ensure that it never happens again.

The Holocaust shows us clearly how horribly destructive hatred and prejudice can be if they remain unchecked. It warns us against the arrogance of those who claim to be superior to others. It alerts us to the dangers when the strong exert uncontrolled power over the weak. The circumstances under which Hitler rose to power in Germany are a reminder of the way in which social and economic hardships can provide opportunities for fanatical leaders to seize power.

The world needs these reminders. Racism still exists, as do intolerance and hatred. **Genocide** continues. So-called "ethnic cleansing" threatens to darken the 21st century as the Holocaust did the 20th. Stories of mass slaughter in horrific circumstances are now quickly relayed around the world. In Bosnia, Kosovo, Africa, and the Middle East, events have come to light that are chilling reminders of the Holocaust. These lessons from the past teach us that only when people learn to live together in mutual respect and understanding will intolerance and inhumanity finally be destroyed.

> *"It requires courage to remember the Holocaust: to squarely face the images of such remorseless evil; to ache for the unconsoled grief of children and parents; to experience the emptiness and loss; to read the unimaginable testimonies to the twisted, vicious inventiveness of the human mind . . ."*
> Simon Wiesenthal

Simon Wiesenthal became famous for his efforts to ensure that Nazi war criminals were brought to justice.

Timeline of the Holocaust

1933 January 30: Hitler comes to power in Germany.
April 1: People are encouraged to boycott Jewish businesses.

1935 September: Nuremberg Laws. These increase persecution of Jews in Germany.

1938 November 9: *Kristallnacht* ("Night of Broken Glass"). Jewish businesses are attacked.

1939 September 3: World War II begins. **Ghettos** established in Polish cities.
May/June: The voyage of the *St. Louis*.

1940 The "euthanasia program" to exterminate the mentally handicapped begins.

1941 Terezin ghetto established outside Prague, Czechoslovakia.
Kovno ghetto in Lithuania also set up.
In eastern Europe the mobile killing squads begin mass killings of Jews.

1942 January 20: The Wannsee Conference takes place near Berlin. The "final solution" is planned and the **death camps** established.
Mass **deportations** of Jews from the ghettos in eastern Europe begins.
Resistance of the Warsaw ghetto to deportations.

1943 April 19: Warsaw ghetto uprising ended. Ghetto is finally destroyed.

1944 May: Deportations from Hungary begin. These are organized from Budapest by Adolf Eichmann.
June 6: D-Day landings in Normandy; the **liberation** of northern Europe began.

1945 May 7: Unconditional surrender by Germany. World War II ends and the camps are liberated. The full extent of the tragedy becomes known.
May–October 1946: Nuremberg Trials of war criminals.

1948 May 14: David Ben-Gurion announces the creation of the state of Israel. The Jews have recovered their ancient homeland but at great cost to the Palestinian Arabs who have lived there for centuries.

1980 The Yad Vahem Memorial Museum founded in Jerusalem.

1993 The United States Memorial Museum and Archives opened in Washington, D.C.

2000 May 2: A Holocaust Remembrance Day observed in the United States and Europe.

More Books to Read

Nonfiction

Boas, Jacob. *We Are the Witnesses: The Diaries of Five Teenagers who Died in the Holocaust.* New York: Henry Holt & Co., 1995.

Byers, Ann. *The Holocaust Camps.* Berkeley Heights, NJ: Enslow Publishers, Inc., 1998.

Fremon, David K. *The Holocaust Heroes.* Berkeley Heights, NJ: Enslow Publishers, Inc., 1998.

Grant, R. G. *The Holocaust.* Austin, Tex.: Raintree Steck-Vaughn, 1998.

Haas, Gerda. *Tracking the Holocaust.* Minneapolis: Lerner, 1995.

Kallen, Stuart A. *The Holocaust.* Edina, Minn.: ABDO, 1994.

Lobel, Anita. *No Pretty Pictures.* New York: Greenwillow Books, 1998.

Mandell, Sherri Lederman. *Writers of the Holocaust.* New York: Facts on File, 1999.

McElroy, Lorie J. *Voices of the Holocaust.* Farmington Hills, Mich.: UXL, 1997.

Opdyke, Irene Gut. *In My Hands: Memories of a Holocaust Rescuer.* New York: Knopf Books for Young Readers, 1999.

Rubin, Susan Goldman. *Fireflies in the Dark: The Story of Freidl Dicker–Brandeis & the Children of Terezin.* New York: Holiday House, Inc., 2000.

Schmittroth, Linda. *People of the Holocaust.* Farmington Hills, Mich.: UXL, 1998

Shuter, Jane. *Auschwitz.* Chicago: Heinemann Library, 1999.

Stranhinich, Helen. *The Holocaust: Understanding and Remembering.* Berkeley Heights, NJ: Enslow Publishers, Inc., 1996.

Fiction

Deedy, Carmen. *The Yellow Star: The Legend of King Christian X of Denmark.* Atlanta, Ga.: Peachtree Publishers, Inc., 2000.

Denenberg, Barry. *One Eye Laughing, the Other Weeping: The Diary of Julie Weiss.* New York: Scholastic, Inc., 2000.

Lowry, Lois. *Number the Stars.* Boston: Houghton Mifflin Company, 1990.

Reiss, Johanna. *The Upstairs Room.* New York: Harper Collins Children's Books, 1972.

Williams, Laura E. *Behind the Bedroom Walls.* New York: Millweed Editions, 1996.

Yolen, Jane. *The Devils Arithmetic.* New York: Penguin, 1990.

Glossary

Allies/Allied forces countries who joined together to defeat Hitler in World War II, 1939–1945

anti-Semitism prejudice or hostility towards Jews

Aryan according to the Nazis, this was the pure German race which was superior to all others in every way

Baltic States countries located on the Baltic Sea—Latvia, Lithuania, and Estonia

boycott refusal to buy goods from a country, a person, or persons

charismatic having the power to charm and inspire devotion

communists people who believe in the ideals of Karl Marx, a German political writer who lived in the 19th century. They claim that property should belong to the state and that each person should only be paid what they needed. This would remove the division between rich and poor.

concentration camp camp in which those who were critical or opposed to a ruling authority were imprisoned

crusades religious wars fought in the Holy Land during the Middle Ages. Christians fought Muslims to remove them from their holy places (places associated with the life of Jesus Christ). The popes of the time also encouraged Christian rulers to remove all non-Christian people in their kingdoms, hence the hostility towards the Jews.

death camp prison camp designed for the purpose of putting people to death

deportees people selected and transported from the ghettos and concentration camps to the death camps for execution

depression economic crisis, resulting in high unemployment

dictator ruler of a state who takes total power and holds onto it by removing any opposition

diplomat person sent by a king, queen, or government to a foreign country to represent the interests of their own country. Diplomats are often involved in discussion and negotiation.

exterminate completely destroy

Feast of the Passover Jewish festival that commemorates the exodus of the Israelites from Egypt, led by Moses

genocide mass killing to exterminate a whole race of people

gentile someone who is not Jewish

ghetto separate part of a city or town, often a slum area, where a minority group of people lived, e.g., the Jews

Hebrew member of the Jewish race which originated in Palestine in ancient times; also the language spoken by these people and used in Israel today

heretic person whose opinion goes against the accepted beliefs of a religion. Often used for those who criticized the Roman Catholic Church, or for those whose religion was outside the Christian Church, such as the Jews.

Inquisition court set up in 15th-century Spain, to root out heretics and make them convert to Christianity. It authorized the use of torture to obtain confessions and sentenced those who would not give up their faith to death by burning.

internment camps camps established to imprison groups of people who are considered undesirable, to remove them from society

lebensraum (room to live) territory claimed by a state as necessary for its survival or growth. Used by the Nazis to justify the invasion of other countries

liberate set free

MI6 British Secret Service organization involved in spying and undercover operations in wartime

National Socialist German Workers Party (Nazis) political party founded in Munich in 1919. Soon after Hitler joined he became its leader. It particularly believed in the superiority of the Aryan race and was opposed to democracy.

neutral not taking sides; term used for a country that does not become involved in a war or in disputes

orator eloquent public speaker

pogrom organized persecution of an ethnic group

propaganda clever advertising or public displays that have the power to affect the way people think

putsch a sudden, violent political revolt

quarantine period of isolation imposed on people who have an infectious disease

rally large gathering of people

refugee person who has fled persecution

Reich former name for the German State. Under the Nazis, Germany was known as the Third Reich

Russian Revolution name for the popular rebellion in Russia in 1917. The czar (emperor) was removed from power, executed, and replaced by the Bolsheviks who introduced a communist government.

scapegoats people who carry the blame for the wrongdoing of others

Slavs groups of people who were native to parts of Russia, Poland, and the former Czechoslovakia

Star of David symbol of the Jewish faith. It is made up of two triangles arranged in such a way as to form a star.

stereotype single, often crude, image or idea used to represent a whole group of people

swastika cross with hooked ends, adopted by Hitler as the symbol of the Nazi party

synagogue Jewish place of worship. It was a very holy place for Jews where they went to be educated in their faith.

Wall Street Crash collapse of the New York Stock Exchange in 1929 brought about by the dramatic fall in the value of shares. It caused serious financial problems in the United States.

Weimar Republic German republic from 1919 until Hitler's accession to power in 1933

Some famous people

Adolf Eichmann Austrian Nazi official. Played a leading role in the organization of the "Final Solution." He escaped to Argentina in 1945, but was tracked down, captured, and executed in Israel in 1962.

Anne Frank Jewish girl born in Germany in 1923, who fled to Holland with her family in 1933. In 1942, following the German invasion of Holland, the family went into hiding. During the next two years, Anne kept a secret diary. In 1944, the family was betrayed and deported to Bergen-Belsen, where Anne died in 1945. After the war, her diary was published. It has made her one of the most well-known figures of the Holocaust.

Index